Trading Analysis

Oscillators for Technical Analysis

By

John Gibson

Copyright 2018 by John Gibson - All rights reserved.

The following book is reproduced below with the goal of providing information that is as accurate and reliable as possible. Regardless, purchasing this book can be seen as consent to the fact that both the publisher and the author of this book are in no way experts on the topics discussed within and that any recommendations or suggestions that are made herein are for entertainment purposes only. Professionals should be consulted as needed prior to undertaking any of the action endorsed herein.

This declaration is deemed fair and valid by both the American Bar Association and the Committee of Publishers Association and is legally binding throughout the United States.

Furthermore, the transmission, duplication or reproduction of any of the following work including specific information will be considered an illegal act irrespective of if it is done electronically or in print. This extends to creating a secondary or tertiary copy of the work or a recorded copy and is only allowed with express written consent from the Publisher. All additional right reserved.

The information in the following pages is broadly considered to be a truthful and accurate account of facts and as such any inattention, use or misuse of the information in question by the reader will render any resulting actions solely under their purview. There are no scenarios in which the publisher or the original author of this work can be in any fashion deemed liable for any hardship or damages that may befall them after undertaking information described herein.

Additionally, the information in the following pages is intended only for informational purposes and should thus be thought of as universal. As befitting its nature, it is presented without assurance regarding its prolonged validity or interim quality. Trademarks that are mentioned are done without written consent and can in no way be considered an endorsement from the trademark holder.

Table of Contents

Introduction 4

Chapter 1: The Commodity Channel Index 8

Chapter 2: The Elder Ray Indicator 25

Chapter 3: The DeMarker Oscillator 41

Chapter 4: The Force Index 53

Chapter 5: William's Percent Range 76

Chapter 6: I've Picked My Indicators. Now What? 88

Introduction

The financial markets have been around in some form or another since before the previous century. They have undergone vast changes, be it in terms of structure or legality or in terms of the underlying participants. The only constant that has remained over all these years has been people's desire to be able to make money from it. Some people choose to invest for the long term, some choose to decode macroeconomic events and some people choose to speculate on the basis of what the markets convey to us about the emotions of those involved with a particular instrument.

These emotions essentially underlie successful trading in more ways than one. A successful trader is able to determine not only the emotions of those trading against her but also determine what emotions are rising up within her at any time when involved in the market. Many traders choose to ignore this basic fact by making systems as mechanical as possible, thinking that a mechanical system will remove the hard work required. This is, of course, a fallacy. Any system, no matter how discretionary it is will require you to master yourself. More than anything else, an investment in this area will bring you more profits than anywhere else. A successful trading system requires you to master 3 elements of trading: Technical, Risk management and mindset.

This book, the second of the series, will take you on a deep dive into the world of oscillators. In the first book, we looked at ever green indicators which inform us of the nature and characteristics of the existing trend. That book ended with a look at the stochastic and RSI oscillators. There are many more oscillators you can use in conjunction with trend indicators to help you decipher the markets though. This book is an attempt to shed some light on and explain the various characteristics and subtleties of some very powerful oscillators so as to enable you to choose which one works best for you. We will be looking at the following indicators in this book:

- The Commodity Channel Index
- The Elder- Ray indicator/ Bulls and Bears power index
- The DeMarker oscillator
- The Force Index
- The Williams percent range

These oscillators offer you the easiest methods of understanding the underlying price action and are the simplest ways of interpreting the markets in conjunction with other trend indicators. Everyday, there's someone, somewhere inventing a new indicator which derives from another existing one with the intention of "fixing" or "optimizing" the older indicator. Such an approach is akin to running an experiment based on false assumptions, receiving useless results and then fixing or improving the experiment method instead of fixing the false assumptions which produced the poor results in the first place!

The correct way to trade successfully is to figure out which indicator fits your mindset profile the best and then let the math work in your favor. You will never have a system that gives you a 100%. The sooner you let go of this assumption the better. You may intellectually know this to be false but ask yourself if your actions communicate the same. For example: do you get frustrated after a loss? This points to a less than perfect understanding of how trading works.

This book will not give you a trading system but will provide you with the components that make up the technical aspect of a full system. Having said that, let's get started!

Chapter 1: The Commodity Channel Index

The commodity channel index or CCI was developed by Donald Lambert in 1980. Lambert, a technical analyst, designed this indicator to predict cyclical turns in commodities. The CCI can be used across all markets though such as the equity, forex and derivatives market and across all instruments like currency pairs, stocks, ETFs, CFDs etc. The indicator has a default input of 14, much like the Stochastic and RSI oscillators we looked at in the previous book, which can be adjusted depending on the time frame you wish to trade in. Wile originally designed to be used to predict long term changes in momentum, the CCI can be used in short term time frames with great success. Generally speaking, the oscillator measures the current price relative to the average trailing price over a given period in the past. This past time period serves as the input for the indicator. When current prices are far above the past, the value is high and conversely low when the current prices are far lower. Like all oscillators the CCI has an overbought and oversold threshold.

The calculation of the CCI is fairly straightforward. The formula is stated below. I've assumed a look back period of 20 for this example. If you choose a different value, the look back period and the SMA value need to be the same when calculating the CCI.

CCI= (Typical Price- 20 SMA of Typical Price)/ (0.015 * Mean Deviation)

Where,

Typical Price= (High+Low+Close)/3

And Mean Deviation is calculated using the below steps,

1. Calculate 20 period SMA of typical price.
2. Calculate each individual typical price within the 20 period.
3. Subtract 1 from each value obtained in 2.
4. Take the absolute value of all the numbers obtained in 3 and sum them up.
5. Divide 4 by 20.

The oscillator fluctuates on either side of 0, with the 100 and -100 levels indicating the overbought and oversold thresholds. Generally speaking a majority of the values will fall below the thresholds with a minority falling past them. These values indicate strength or weakness in the market price for that instrument. A shorter look back period will cause greater volatility and more spikes into the overbought or oversold zones while a larger value will result in a greater smoothing of the curve. Like always, I recommend traders play around with the values they feel the most comfortable with. Resist the temptation to turn this into a game of deciphering the exact value of the look back period. From an overall strategy point of view, the look back period does not matter as much as you would think.

The CCI is a versatile oscillator in that in can be interpreted in a variety of ways. Generally speaking, positive values indicate strength compared to the past and negative values indicate weakness compared to the past. A surge of value over 100 indicates massive strength and may signal the start of a bull trend while a plunge below -100 may signal the start of a bear trend. The CCI can also be used as a leading indicator in a mean reversion strategy and the overbought and oversold levels can be used as a signal to enter in the direction of the mean. I understand not all of you might be familiar with the basics of a mean reversion strategy so I'll detail this in the next paragraph. Those familiar with this may safely skip to the next one.

Certain instruments behave in a largely predictable manner where the average price over a given period advances or declines by a fixed percentage. The S&P 500 over this past decade has exhibited this tendency, for example. For such instruments, employing a strategy known as mean reversion is a safe way to ensure profits. Essentially, the strategy bets that the average price for a period will always revert to the historic mean. So if the average price over a given period is above the trailing mean, a short trade will be placed with the belief that price will revert to the usual average. Similarly a long will be initiated if price is below the historic mean. As is evident, this strategy needs to be employed over a long period to see any success. What might not be as apparent is that the strategy also needs to be applied on either a higher time frame or a lower time frame to succeed. What I mean is, applying it on a daily or a 15 minute time frame generally gives the best results. An in between time frame like the 60 minute, which is a higher time frame for a large number of traders as well as a lower time frame for a large number, doesn't really product the same results. So using the CCI, which indicates overbought or oversold levels, we can time our entry into the market in the belief that the market will change direction soon. Personally, I've found this strategy most appealing to those who are comfortable with mathematics and like experimenting with quantitative strategies. Being more of a visual person, my preference is price action which I've detailed in my other books, and this strategy has never been a major part of my toolbox.

Most traders would think the overbought or oversold levels would be the easiest way to trade this indicator. Buy when the oscillator dips below -100 and sell when it goes past 100. Most traders also happen to lose money in the markets. The CCI is an unbound oscillator, meaning there is no theoretical upper or lower limit for it. When the oscillator was first designed, this was a viable strategy but with it being in use for over 30 years now, this strategy will not work simply because everyone else in the market is aware of it. Instead, fading or doing the opposite of this original strategy will give you a lot of gains and enable you to profit from the mistakes of other traders who do not understand this indicator. As a general rule, buy when the indicator goes past 100 and sell when the indicator goes below -100. Ensure that the price and indicator converge, meaning, if the CCI dips below -100, price is making new lows as well. If there is a divergence, then do not trade this particular strategy. Stop loss levels can be placed using basic support and resistance methods (see my other books for a detailed analysis of support and resistance) and aim for a reward of at least 2R (R being the percent of your account you risk per trade) with this method. A great optimizer of this strategy is to look at the slope of the oscillator line as it goes past the levels. The steeper the slope of price and the oscillator line, the better your odds of profit.

A word of caution. The above strategy needs to be aligned with the trend of the current market. In other words you need to be aware of what the prevailing market trend is. If the market is in a downtrend and you see the oscillator break the 100 level to the upside, no matter the slope of the line, this is not a signal for you to go long. Similarly, in an uptrend a break below -100 is not a signal to go short. Trading blindly like this is an indication that you're looking for a shortcut or some secret to unlock the markets. Such a situation does not exist and you need to stop thinking in this way. Learn the proper way to trade and see your profits multiply more than you can ever imagine. The correct situation to look for a bullish signal using this method is to see if the market is trending upwards in a small manner. Then if the oscillator breaks the 100 level to the upside, it means bullish strength is increasing and it is safe to go long. Similarly look for a slight bearish trend when looking for a break of -100 to the downside. Needless to say, do not use this strategy in a range. If you have trouble determining the trend or range condition of the market, you can use a trend momentum indicator like the ADX or any other indicator I detailed in the previous book of this series. Used in conjunction like this, you will have a clearer picture of the market.

In a ranging market, where the boundaries are well respected, it makes sense to apply the overbought/oversold limits as originally intended. More often than not, in a prolonged range, we will see the CCI value go past the limits near the range boundary. There is a caveat though to this. The CCI, being an unbound oscillator, will print different values at the range limit for different instruments. More volatile instruments will have a higher value when the price is near the limits of the range. Therefore, instead of blindly buying the -100 breach and selling the 100 upside break, note the historic levels which the indicator printed near the range limits. When price reaches the range limit, check to see if the same value is printed by the oscillator. If so, enter in the appropriate direction (short if near the top of the range, long if near the bottom) and ride price all the way back to the opposite range limit.

Another way of using the CCI is to use it in conjunction with another oscillator like the stochastic and use it to trade convergences on small time frames. This approach will be better illustrated in the charts that follow this chapter but for now its enough for you to grasp the basics of this strategy. This will work only on the 15 minute and lower time frames and the holding period for this strategy will usually be less than 20 minutes. As such its ideal for traders who are looking to day trade or implement a strategy that is short term in nature but not as short term as scalping. Due to the short holding times, the price execution becomes important and due to this reason I would advise against using this in a developed market with a centralized order book, like a stock market, due to the presence of HFT firms. Using this in a market with very low HFT presence, like say the Chinese or Indian stock market, or in a decentralized market, like forex, is the best way to go. The way the entry signal works is this: We watch for a convergence of the CCI and the Stochastic. If the CCI, for example, bounces up from the -100 (oversold) level and the Stochastic displays a bullish crossover as well, we go long on the close of the bar. Our stop will be placed on the basis of S/R levels and our exit signal is when the stochastic indicator displays a bearish signal. Please note: we need both indicators to confirm our entry signal but only one to generate an exit signal. The indicators will not always move in sync so its important to check the condition of both of them if one of them is generating an entry signal. As I mentioned previously, the charts following this chapter will illustrate this technique clearly.

Another useful way of using the CCI is to deploy it across two time frames. On the higher time frame, look for the CCI to move above 100 or below -100. This indicates a longer term bullish or bearish trend respectively. Then, switching to the lower time frame, as long as the value in the higher time frame remains beyond those thresholds, look for the CCI to cross above -100 or below 100 respectively. For example, if the higher time frame CCI is above +100, then we go down to the lower time frame and observe the CCI there. We wait for the moment the lower time frame CCI breaks the -100 line to the upside. Similarly, if the higher time CCI is below -100, we wait for the lower time frame CCI to break below 100. This break on the lower time frame is our entry signal. Set your stop loss on the basis of support and resistance and exit for a reward of at least 2R. The logic behind this strategy is to take advantage on a lower time frame pullback of a well established trend on the higher time frame. Needless to say, this strategy will not work if you deploy it in ranging conditions. A good optimizer of this method is to use a trend strength indicator (like the ones covered in the previous book) to ascertain the probability of the trend lasting. It is always a good idea to use two indicators which measure different aspects of the market to help develop a more rounded picture.

The charts on the following pages will illustrate the use of the CCI.

The chart above is of the GBPJPY currency pair on the 60 minute time frame. The vertical lines illustrate both long and short opportunities available as the CCI crosses the 100 to the upside (long) and -100 to the downside (short).

Most of these trades will result in a profit of at least 2R irrespective of the session or time of the day (FX is a 24 hour market). This shows the versatility of this indicator and strategy. Notice how frequently the indicator gives you a signal. This means even if you miss a signal overnight there's always a chance to get back in. This is just the number of signals over a few days and the signals are time stamped so you can check it out for yourself. Remember to take at least a 2R profit target for your trades and place your stop at a logical S/R level. This will increase your holding time in some cases but better a longer holding time than risk an unnecessary loss. Those unfamiliar with S/R principles can refer my book on Forex Trading for an in depth discussion on the to

The USDSGD on the 5 minute chart illustrates yet another strategy which can be implemented using the CCI. Here in conjunction with the stochastic oscillator, we look for a convergence to take advantage of small price movements.

Our entry signal to go long is an upward break of the -100 on the CCI AND a bullish crossover on the stochastic (solid line over dashed). Our short entry signal is a downward break of the 100 level on the CCI AND a bearish crossover on the stochastic (dashed over solid). The exit signal for a long position is a bearish crossover on the stochastic and for a short position, we exit when the stochastic displays a bullish crossover. The entries we receive over a period of little under 4 hours is marked by the vertical lines. A long position is denoted by the arrows under the bar while a short position is indicated by the arrow above it. A profitable exit is indicated by a check mark on the exit bar and a loss by a cross over it. Let's walk through this chart briefly.

At the first vertical line, we see the CCI has broken over the -100 level and the stochastic has also completed a bullish crossover. This is our signal to go long and we do so as close to the closing price of the bar. We place our stop below the prior swing low. We now wait for an exit signal which is a bearish crossover of the stochastic. Within 20 minutes we receive this signal and exit for a profit. We can book approximately 1.5R as profit on this position.

The second vertical line gives us our second entry signal and this time its a short signal. The CCI has broken under the 100 level and the stochastic has completed a bearish crossover. Our stop is placed above the prior swing high and we wait for our exit signal which arrives a few bars later. We book another 1.5-1.7R as profit. Thus far, we're up 3R on the day. Not bad for an hour's work.

No time to gloat though as we immediately receive yet another entry signal to go long. This time we can take a really tight stop since we're almost at the swing low. Price bounces to the prior swing high and we promptly receive another exit signal. This time our profit is around 2R. We're up 5R thus far on the day.

Our next entry is a while coming and again is a long position. This is a brief position and the profit on this amounts to slightly more than break even. The next entry signal is a short one and this position ends up costing us a little less than a -1R loss. Our stop would have been placed over the bar we entered on and we luckily received an exit signal before price hit the stop. We currently have an open position using this strategy as we come to the end of the chart. Our overall results are a profit of little under 5R. If we were risking 1% of our account, we've just cleared 5% in a few hours.

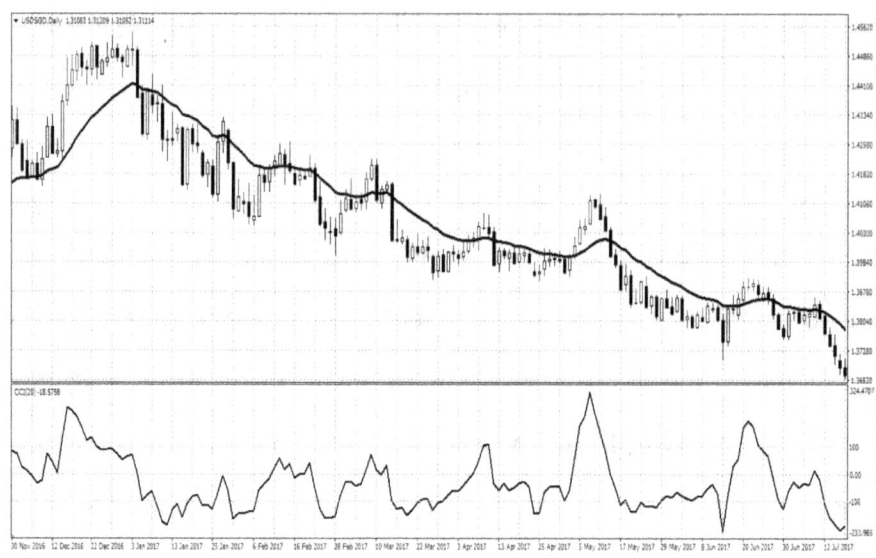

The above chart shows the folly of using the CCI as per the original strategy of buying when it goes over 100 and selling when below -100. The strategy has been around for many years now and there's no profit to be made in doing what everyone else is doing. You're better off fading this strategy. Looking at the chart above, doing the exact opposite would have resulted in a tidy profit on the USDSGD pair.

This concludes our look at the CCI. Up next, we will go in depth into the Elder Ray indicator also known as the bulls/bears power index.

Chapter 2: The Elder Ray Indicator

The Elder Ray indicator was developed by Dr Alexander Elder and introduced in his famous book "Trading for a Living" in 1989. This is yet another indicator which has been around for many years now and is one of those evergreen ones which are versatile and have withstood the many changes the market has undergone. Dr. Elder named the indicator as such by likening it to an X-Ray on the markets. The indicator itself uses 3 components: Bulls power, bears power and a 13 period EMA. The idea is to ascertain the relative strength of the bulls and bears by digging deeper into the market and going past the superficial. The indicator fleshes out the price signifying maximum bull power and maximum bear power while using the 13 period EMA as a consensus between the two parties. It then measures the probability of the bulls or bears pushing past their respective maximum prices. The balance between bulls and bears is important and any changes in this balance usually signifies changes in trend.

The indicator works as any other oscillator would, pin pointing areas of extreme pessimism or optimism. The oscillator components are labeled "Bull power" and "Bear power" respectively. The components are calculated as follows:

Bull Power= Current high price- 13 period EMA

Bears Power= Current low price- 13 period EMA

Under usual circumstances, the bull power will be positive and bears power will be negative. If the values flip from their usually expected state, this means the opposite side has gained control over the market. That is, if the bull power is negative the bears have overcome the bulls. If bears power is positive, it means the bulls have overcome the bears (Remember that the bears power is usually negative). Generally, one should avoid going long if the bear power is positive or short if the bull power is negative. The biggest difficult traders have in applying this indicator is that it requires you to customize your trading platform as not many have the indicator built in. Most platforms though do have the bulls power and bears power histograms represented as separate windows. You will need to plot the 13 period EMA on your chart and analyze the three windows simultaneously. This does sound like a pain but once you practice this method, you won't notice it anymore. Providing the actual script is beyond the scope of this book since 1) I'm not a programmer and 2) You can always hire one or search on the web for a script someone else has coded for your platform. This is why the charts at the end of this chapter will look different from usual representations of the Elder Ray you will find from other sources. I've taken the most commonly available form and displayed it here so as to have maximum relevance.

Now that that little detail is out of the way, let's look at some strategies. This indicator doesn't lend itself to a wide variety of strategies since it measures something very specific. Generally speaking, like all indicators, it works best in environments where the trend strength is high. In a range, as I've mentioned previously, the best course of action is to simply trade the range boundaries and not use any indicators. For a more detailed look at trend strength and its interpretation, please refer to my series of books titled "forex trading" and "day trading". This indicator is best used to spot reversals in the trend. Now I do not recommend beginner's go around hunting for trend reversals since this is a very advanced skill and it takes extreme mental strength to do the opposite. Instead, I suggest you trade the pullbacks within a trend, that is, wait for the indicator to signal to you when a pullback or complete and then enter in the direction of the larger trend. One of the reasons many traders shun this indicator is because they make the mistake of trying to catch the exact moment when the trend reverses. This is the wrong way to use it. Ideally, your trades should mostly be with trend. The best way to do this is to pin point the end of the counter trend movement (pullbacks or rallies) and then enter in the original trend's direction. It is very important for you to grasp this and it will make the biggest difference to your trading results.

The simplest rules of this strategy are as follows:

1) Note the slope of the EMA. Is it up, down or sideways. Ideally, you want it to be up or down in a definitive manner.

If sideways, just stay out. Th direction of the EMA slope determines the direction we will look to enter.

2) For a long position, the Bear power should be decreasing over time if in negative territory or positive.

3) For a short position, the bull power needs to be decreasing over time if positive or should be in negative territory.

You will find variations of this strategy which will call for the bear power or bull power to be in a specific position, that is below or above zero or some such. It is my opinion that this merely complicates things and the key to trading this indicator well is to keep things simple. There are optimizers for this strategy but again, a successful strategy is about identifying what element contributes the most to your results. In this case, the best optimizer is the EMA slope. Unfortunately there isn't any specific reading which will gives us the ideal slope. You will need to practice extensively and get comfortable with the degree of slope which gives you the best results. Do not get caught up trying to determine if the previous two bars have been rising or falling or some such nonsense. Making this system even more mechanical is running away from the major issue, which is, you need to put in the work to be successful. No magic indicator exists which will unlock market secrets.

Advanced or experienced traders can consider adding further two rules regarding pyramiding their position. Again, the specifics of pyramiding is beyond the scope of this book since it involves your trading plan. I'll explore this in great detail in my other books. As such, I advise beginners to stay away from pyramiding. With this strategy it isn't something essential to your success. The rules for pyramiding are:

1) Add to your long position when the bears power dips below 0 and crosses back up.

2) Similarly add to your shorts when the bull power goes above 0 and crosses back below.

Whether pyramiding or placing a lone trade, you will enter at the close of the bar where the entry signal is observed. Your stop needs to be placed at a logical S/R level and you must take a reward of at least 2R (R being the percent of your account you risk per trade). An optional screen you can add to this strategy is to determine the trend on the higher time frame chart and trade the lower one. This is a decent optimizer but in my opinion, you'd be better off just using a trend indicator, like the ones I've already covered in the previous book, to help you determine trend strength. If you build your skill level up with regards to the EMA slope, you won't need a trend indicator of course.

The charts on the following pages will illustrate this strategy in action.

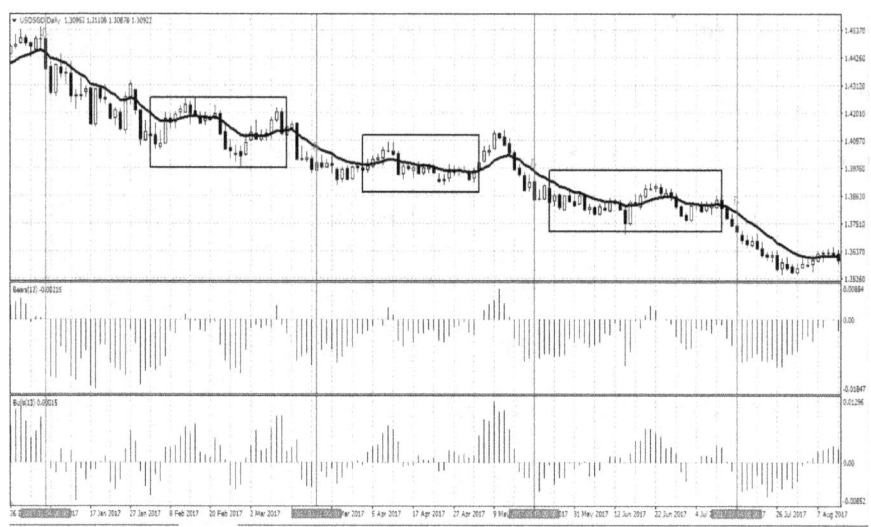

One of the biggest difficulties traders face when using the Elder Ray is deciding what is an appropriate time to start paying attention to the indicator in anticipation of an entry signal. Generally speaking, there are 2 situations or conditions you need to keep in mind to help you out with this. The first is after a reversal has occurred in trend, look for price to break decisively below the EMA. A trend reversal, which I do not recommend, beginners trade, is usually characterized by a prolonged decrease of the prevailing trend strength, that is, if in a bull trend, the bull power will steadily decrease over time and will diverge from price while simultaneously the bears power will increase. I will delve into this in a later chart but for now, lets just note that a reversal has occurred on the far left of this chart and price has decisively broken below the EMA.

Once this break happens, we notice that that bull power has declined significantly. This fulfills our condition for a short position and we duly enter at the close with the stop above the swing high. This beings me to the second situation one must look at in anticipation of a signal: The slope of the EMA. Notice how a few bars after entering our position price breaks above the EMA briefly. Now, a trader inexperience in dealing with this indicator would have thought this would be a great time to evaluate whether a long position is on. Look at the slope of the EMA though. It is firmly pointed downwards. As such, there is no need to go looking for a long in this scenario so you might as well save yourself the time. Price then starts moving sideways (indicated by the first rectangular box) and the EMA reflects this. Remember that, ideally, we want our EMA to have a well defined slope upwards or downwards. It is neither up nor down decisively here so we stay out.

After this, price decisively moves down along with the EMA and we can now being to look for shorts. We spot an opportunity soon after it breaks to the downside and notice that bull power has decreased drastically. The entry is indicated by the second vertical line. A small note on the decreasing bull power: The decrease in bull or bear power needs to be evaluated over a number of bars, not just the recent few ones. Here, we see when we look at the bull power over the past few bars, it has decreased drastically. Looking over a longer period though, it seems like the bull power is staying largely consistent with a few dips below the zero level. When I mentioned previously that the bull power has decreased, I was referring to the longer term view. The bull power to the left of this chart is not shown, since there's only so much I can highlight, but it represents a major decrease in bull power. I'll highlight the price action to the left of this chart in the next image where I will discuss spotting trend reversals. So once again, I've made the conclusion of decreasing bull power on the basis of values you cannot see on this particular chart but can see on the next one.

Price again goes into a sideways movement with the EMA going flat. This is indicated by the second rectangular box. As such, we want to stay patient during such moments. More advanced traders can dive into a lower time frame and try to trade this range in the direction of the trend. I recommend you try this only once you've stabilized your results using some basic strategies first though. Price after the box does something interesting. It breaks past the EMA strongly and the bears power decreases and bull power increases which leads us to question whether there will be a reversal. As we will understand on the next chart, such action is not a reversal and once we've ascertained this, we go back to trying to enter the bear trend and pin point the end of this particular rally. Our conclusion is soon proved right as price dips back below the EMA and the bull power decreases drastically once more. This entry is indicated by the third vertical line.

Price then goes sideways once more and eventually gives us one final entry at the right extreme of the chart. Following the thought process thus far illustrated, see if you can spot the entry signal. I recommend covering this chart with a piece of paper and following along and trying to trade this chart using this system yourself. This is the best way for you to learn. Please note: this method requires a lot of practice since it requires you to interpret not one or two but three separate elements of the charts. Initially you will struggle and you will pick up a lot of false signals. The key to learning this is to stay calm and keep your expectations in check. This ties directly to the topic of risk management and mindset in trading which I'll briefly go over in the final chapter but its something I've mentioned in my previous book as well with regards to developing an entire trading system. For now, ensure you practice as much as possible and do not expect every single trade to end up in profit. There is no system which will give you this so you might as well drop this expectation now.

Now, let's look at the same instrument but shift the chart slightly to the left so as to understand the process of a trend reversal better and how to interpret them. The next chart illustrates this method.

Generally when deciding to enter a long position we tend to look at the bear power characteristics and when looking to go short we look at the bull power characteristics. When we look for confirmation of a reversal though, we flip this around. That is in case of a bull trend turning bearish, we look at the bull power and in case of a bear trend turning bullish, we look at the bear power. Please note: the entry signals to go short or long remain the same. The reversal by itself is not an entry signal, you still need to fulfill the entry requirements previously mentioned.

The above chart is the same as the previous one just shifted to the left a bit. Here we see the bull trend reverses into the bear trend we previously traded. Prior to the reversal, on the left off the chart, notice how the price makes new highs but the bull power remains exactly the same. This action is denoted by the successively higher circles on the price chart and the rectangle at the same level on the bulls power chart. Note also how the previous swing high corresponded with a higher high on the bull power chart as well. This latest action then is a divergence and is a clear signal the bull power is unsustainable and a reversal must be expected soon.

Similarly, on the right side of the chart, you will recall the moment when price broke through quite strongly past the EMA (last circle on the right half of the chart). I mentioned then that this was not a price reversal. Can you see why? Look at this swing high compared to the previous swing high (also circled) and compare the bulls power level to each other. You will see another divergence here but not in favor of the bulls. The bulls power is printing a higher value but the price is far below the previous swing high. Also, to look for a bullish reversal, that is a bear trend ending, we need to look at the bears power, not the bulls power. Now the bear power is decreasing here but there isn't enough of a divergence from the price levels to justify an existence of a trend reversal.

This judgment I've just made is a qualitative one and it comes from experience trading the markets. This is why I've repeatedly said you need to practice this strategy extensively before using it. There are qualitative aspects to this which can be developed only through repetition. If you feel uncomfortable with this aspect of the strategy, I recommend you pick another indicator which is more clear cut. After all, trading successfully is about picking the strategy that fits YOU the best.

This concludes our look at the Elder Ray indicator. Used correctly, this is extremely powerful but it does require you to make qualitative judgments which not everyone will be comfortable with.

Next we take a look at another great indicator: The DeMarker Oscillator

Chapter 3: The DeMarker Oscillator

The DeMarker indicator (DeM) is a relatively less used oscillator compared to some of the more classical indicators. Developed by technical analyst Tom DeMarker, the indicator attempts to measure the demand for a currency pair and assesses the directional bias of the market. It functions and looks much like any other oscillator with overbought and oversold levels identifying areas of trend exhaustion. The indicator is based on relative price data so while it was originally developed using daily price bars, it is applicable across all time frames. Instruments wise, technically speaking it is applicable across the board but my personal experience has been that it works best on currency pairs. While the exact mechanics of this is not known to me, suffice to say that I'd recommend you use this for trading FX pairs. If you do plan on using it on any other instrument, such as stocks, I recommend back testing it extensively through at least two market cycles. So as of writing this book, that means you back test it starting from the market recovery following the dot com bubble, through the bull market, the credit crisis and the massive bull market recovery that followed. Using this in a less developed market might also be a good play but as always, test the strategy extensively before committing to it live.

Like other oscillators the DeM is most effective when combined with another indicator which measure a different aspect of the market, like trend. While combining this with something like the Ichimoku cloud is a bit pointless, since the Ichimoku is pretty substantial in and as of itself, the ADX and Bollinger bands work quite well with this oscillator. Physically, the oscillator is represented much like others but instead of a 100 or -100, this oscillator moves between 0 and 1 with levels drawn at 0.7 and 0.3. There are some variations which plot -100 and 100 but don't be alarmed when you see this, the logic is essentially the same, the values are just normalized differently. The values are calculated as below:

1) Choose input period. Default is 14. Lower values make the indicator more sensitive.

2) Calculate DeMax. Value is 0 if Current High- Previous High is <0. If > 0, then DeMax= Current High- Previous High.

3) Calculate DeMin. If Previous low- Current low >0 then =DeMin, else DeMin=0.

4) DeM= SMA of DeMax/(SMA of DeMax+SMA of DeMin)

As should be obvious, calculating this value by hand is a bit of a pain but any charting software can accomplish this easily. As can be seen from the calculation, the indicator essentially compares the current high/low with the previous high or low and thus determines the general direction of the market. A series of increasing DeMax values point to increasing bullishness while decreasing DeMin values point to increasing bearishness. A longer period will smooth out any fluctuations as is the case with any oscillator. This brings me to an important, if somewhat digressive, point. The underlying logic of every type of indicator is the same no matter how it is calculated, whether the calculation is simple or complex or derived from another indicator or from price. It is important you recognize this because traders often get caught up with their bad results and end up thinking changing an indicator will answer their woes. This is not the case. You need to choose whichever indicator you're the most comfortable with, since every indicator will have its own quirks, and then stick to that strategy and see if it fits your risk personality. Only if it doesn't, you move on. There is no perfect indicator as some gurus will have you believe. If you take nothing else from this book, learn this point. Trading successfully is far more than just finding the perfect indicator. In face trading is not at all about finding a perfect indicator. Such an indicator does not exist. Pick one you're comfortable with and then work on your risk management and mindset.

Some of the quirks of this indicator is that it sometimes functions as a leading indicator. I personally feel it functions as a leading indicator right up until the point you start trusting it with your positions in the market. As such, I'd advise you use it as a part of the strategies I'll shortly highlight. The DeM also tends to pick bottoms better than tops. One reason for this is that there is usually greater institutional and professional presence when a market bottoms out or gets bearish. This produces much sharper price action and thus the indicator picks this up well. Bullish moves tend to run longer than expected due to greater presence of inexperienced traders who mostly think the market ought to only go up and never down. This produces smoother peaks as the price heads upwards. Some traders add an EMA onto the price chart to get a better picture of the market. The reason is, as I mentioned before, when the market heads upwards, the DeM tends to produce some divergences from price. Sometimes, these divergences act as leading indicators and sometimes, its just a false signal. Having an EMA gives a better indicator of which way the market is currently headed. If you wish to use a strategy different from the ones I've highlighted next, my recommendation is to use an EMA on the price chart to clear things up a bit for you.

The DeM is not used extensively compared to some of the more classic oscillators. Due to this reason, the number of strategies that it can be employed in is low. This is not a bad thing since its a clear indication that a simple strategy works. Generally, the greater the number of strategies an indicator is involved in, the less effective it is since its mechanisms have been rumbled upon by other traders. One example of a simple strategy involving the DeM is to use it as an oscillator is intended to be used along with the 20 EMA. A long signal is generated when the DeM crosses the 0.3 line from below (that is breaks above 0.3) and the corresponding price bar also breaks above the 20 EMA. A short signal is generated when the DeM crosses the 0.7 level from above (that is breaks below 0.7) and the corresponding price bar also breaks below the 20 EMA. You will sometimes see that the price bar is already below or above the EMA as the DeM crosses its respective levels. This is a legitimate signal. However, price crossing the EMA AFTER the DeM has crossed its levels is not a legitimate entry. Price needs to move below/above the 20 EMA either with or before the DeM crosses the 0.7 or 0.3 levels. The position is exited at either a 2R reward or the DeM crossing into the opposite threshold, whichever comes first. That is, if price hits the 2R level first, that is your exit. If however, before reaching the 2R level in a long position, the DeM moves into oversold territory (crossing 0.7) and crosses back below it, that would be your exit point. Similarly, the exit for a short position would be when the DeM moves below the 0.3 level and crosses back up above it. As always, enter and exit at the bar close.

Like all oscillators, the DeM can be used as part of a simple divergence strategy. The strategy with this indicator is doubly effective however due to the relatively smaller number of traders using it. Thus any entry signal you receive is extremely strong. In fact, with this strategy you do not need to use any other indicator. A word of caution though: No strategy remains a secret for long and will be rumbled eventually. Due to this, it is is important you keep a keen eye on the statistics of this strategy from a risk management perspective. The divergence strategy, as the name suggests is when you see the DeM and price print diverging conditions or slopes. For example, if price prints a higher low but the DeM prints a lower low, that is a divergence. Stops can be placed on the basis of simple S/R principles and target a reward of at least 2R for your trades. Experienced traders can trail their stops as they wish. It is necessary though to evaluate the context in which the divergence occurs. Due to this reason, this is a more discretionary strategy than the previous one detailed and traders who prefer a fully mechanical strategy might not prefer this. The charts on the following pages illustrate the strategies.

On the GBPJPY currency pair we see the results of the mechanical strategy first discussed. We enter long as DeM moves above the 0.3 line and price either previously or simultaneously moves above the 20 EMA. A short position is initiated when the DeM moves below the 0.7 level and price either previously or simultaneously moves below the 20 EMA.

The vertical lines denote the entry bars and the exits are noted by the cross marks above them, irrespective of profit or loss. As you can also see, this is the H1 time frame which shows that this indicator can be used successfully across all time frames. The exits shown are only on the basis of following the exit rule whereby we use the DeM only for exit, not the 2R take profit level. This is because stop loss levels will vary for all traders and it is not possible to estimate the 2R level.

As such, we can see that we start off slow early in the month but by month's end we have an open trade that is significantly in profit which has put us well into the green and wiped out any losses that might have occurred. That's not to say many losses occurred. We start off with a break even trade followed by a loss (which hits a logical stop loss level), followed by 2 small wins, a big win and an ongoing open trade which is well in profit.

The H1 time frame for the NZDUSD above also illustrates the profitability of this strategy. In extremely volatile price action, which would produce extreme results in most strategies, we can see above that we make a decent profit following this strategy. The exact results will depend on your stop loss levels but generally speaking this strategy does give us positive results.

In the chart above we see a positive divergence between the DeM and price. Price is in a downtrend which is getting more volatile and right on cue, the DeM prints a higher low which price makes a lower low. A few things to note before you implement this strategy: This is a very subjective way of trading the markets. You will note that I mentioned price was in a downtrend that was becoming more and more volatile. This is an example of reading the context in which the market is. I was aware of the fact that I need to look for a reversal which seemed probable. It was only after this that I started looking for potential divergences.

Blindly trading every single divergence will only result in losses. You need to be able to read basic price action before using this very powerful strategy. Those interested can refer to by books in day trading and forex trading to understand price action and order flow mechanics.

This concludes our look at the very powerful Demarker oscillator. Next up, we look at the Force Index, another relatively less used oscillator.

Chapter 4: The Force Index

The oscillators we've looked at thus far can be applied to all kinds of markets, be it FX, stocks, bond or derivative. This particular oscillator though relies on volume and as such, is most effective in the stock markets or any market where volume data can be relied upon. Therefore, this indicator isn't very effective in FX markets because those do not have a centralized order book. Nonetheless, the Force Index is an extremely useful indicator both by itself and when combined with a trend measuring indicator. Developed by Dr. Alexander Elder and introduced in his book, Trading for a Living, the Force Index aims to measure the power of the bulls behind an uptrend and that of the bears behind every downtrend.

The philosophy of this indicator is simple. There are three essential elements to any movement of a stock: Extent, or length of the move, direction of price change and volume. These three elements are combined to form an oscillator which fluctuates between positive and negative territory. The originally stated use of this indicator was to determine the direction of the overall trend, forecast reversals via divergences and identify corrections in the trend which can enable us to get on board with the trend. While not all of these strategies work these days due to this indicator being extensively used, there are many other ways in which you can use this oscillator and it is worth studying this and adding it to your trading toolbox.

Visually, the force index is represented as fluctuating above and below zero. It is above zero when the bulls are in control and below when the bears are in control. The calculation of the force index involves calculating two components named the Force (1) and Force (13). In other words, the force index for 1 period and the 13 period force index. The calculation is as follows:

Force(1)= (Current close- prior close)* volume

Force(13)= 13 period EMA of Force (1)

The volume influences the values of the force index as is obvious to see. A large move on small volume will result in a small value for the indicator whereas a larger volume will give higher values. A positive value is obtained when the current close is above the previous one and negative when the current close is lesser than the previous bar. The raw value of the oscillator is plotted as a histogram with the center line as zero. The values are then plotted on the positive or negative side as appropriate and the curve is smoothed by using an EMA (I've used 13 in the calculation above). Technically you can use even a 2 day EMA but for practical purposes, a value above 10 is ideal.

When there is little volume or price movement, the indicator will hover around zero indicating low momentum currently present. Therefore in small ranges, one often sees such values printing. Needless to say, you want to avoid using this indicator or indeed trading when price is in a range. As explained earlier and in my previous books, the best way to trade a range is to buy the lows and sell the highs. Only novices try to trade the middle and end up losing money as a result. Another point of importance that needs to be highlighted is that most traders, especially those trading the stock market, tend to fall in to the trap of trying to determine the perfect value for the number of EMA periods this indicator requires. I urge you to recognize the folly of this method of thinking and to fix your mindset and expectations with regards to trading and the process of doing so successfully. The correct way to approach this is to play around with the values and find one that is "good enough" as opposed to perfect. Perfection does exist in the markets but not in the way you think. I'll cover all of this in my book on trading mindset but for now just remember to avoid this trap.

The interpretation of the oscillator is quite straight forward. A positive value implies buyers were stronger than sellers and a negative one implies the opposite, that is, sellers stronger than buyers. The extent of price change gives us the distance price moved and can be seen as a proxy for the strength of buying or selling behind the move. Either way a large change between closing prices is something of note and this indicator perfectly captures it. The volume is a direct representation of the commitment, as Elder put it, of the players behind the move. A big move on a small volume is less reliable than a big move with a large number of players behind it. Those of you who are familiar with volume spread analysis will recognize the principle in play here. (For a discussion of the VSA strategy refer to my book Day Trading:

Trade the Stock Market Like a Pro). The Force index manages to quantify all these elements into one chart and reading.

One of the uses of this indicator is to determine long term trend. A shorter time period will produce a more jagged, volatile curve whereas a lot of smoothing will occur over a larger time period. Traders most often use a 100 day period for the force index to determine long term trend changes and patterns. A crossover from below, that is from negative to positive, indicates a change from bearish to bullish and a crossover from above indicates a trend change to bearish from bullish. Once again, this is applicable only for longer time periods and on higher time frames. It doesn't make sense to try and spot long term trend characteristics on the 15 minute chart while using a look back period of 20. General advice is to use a 100 period look back period and the daily chart and above for this case.

The force index is most useful when day trading in my personal experience. When combined with some form of trend identification, a short term force index reading can be used to enter in the trend direction and take advantage of the end of small corrections. What I mean is, in an uptrend, for example, when a pullback occurs, a short term force index indicator will dip below zero due to its sensitivity. When it crosses back up above zero is when you enter in the trend direction. You can use an indicator that measure trend strength or direction like the ADX, Bollinger bands or EMAs or you can visually look at the trend. Another method is to use a higher period force index on the higher time frame and then trade the lower one with the lower look back period. Generally, I'd advise you to use a different indicator since its best to gather confirmation from multiple sources before trade entry. Traders can modulate the number of entries and activity level this strategy will produce by playing with the look back period on the indicator. Again, its essential to find a period which suits you the best, given your risk tolerance and cognitive loading abilities, as opposed to trying to find something that works "all the time" in the market. Practice using different values and go with the one that feels the easiest and makes you the most money on paper. For this strategy, do not trade counter trend and aim for a profit target of at least 2R or exit when the oscillator crosses over to the other side of the zero line, which ever comes first. So in a long position, you take your reward at either 2R or when the force index crosses into negative territory. Place your stop loss on the basis of S/R principles, that is either below or above swings or obvious S/R levels.

Another interesting way to use this indicator is to take advantage of its extreme readings. Now, ideally this strategy should not produce signals with great frequency, perhaps once a day if you're day trading, and generally I'd advise you to stay away from volatile stocks and instruments if you're using this strategy. The reason this strategy is effective is because of the volume component present in its calculation. When a stock or instrument experiences a volume spike, no matter the price direction, the value of the force index shoots up to an extreme value. Usually we'll see this then oscillate back down to more normal levels until the indicator reaches its prior low or high levels. The entry signal is when the indicator bounces up or down from the prior low or high. We enter on the close of that price bar and ride it for at least a 2R profit. While I appreciate this strategy is a bit difficult to understand in words, the charts at the end of this chapter will illustrate this method perfectly.

Like all other oscillators, the force index exhibits divergences from price. Unlike other oscillators though, I would caution you against trading a divergence. This might seem a contradiction since in the previous chapter on the Demarker indicator, I listed a divergence strategy. Well, the Demarker has the advantage of not being as widely used and relatively new to the scene compared to the Force index. The divergence strategy is something which was first proposed by Elder in his book and many traders have since jumped on the band wagon and the strategy has been played to death. While I wouldn't advocate fading a divergence since that would be too risky, I would stay away from trading one since there's too much noise involved with every trader out there looking to get in on the action.

Combining the Force index with another oscillator works quite well but the best way of using this is to combine it with a trend indicator of some sort like the ADX or MACD. Again, its always better to have your entry signal confirmed by two separately derived indicators. There are some systems which choose to combine this with the RSI or Stochastic oscillator but I'm not keen on this since most of these systems are extremely mechanical and rely on a myriad of rules. Most traders will find that such systems work for a short while and then suddenly stop working because they were based on a quirk of the market which the system unearthed through pure luck. I'm mentioning this because you need to stay away from the temptation of thinking complex is better. The reality is the simpler your system is, the more successful you'll be. Limit yourself to two indicators at most and learn them inside out. It pays far more to use an indicator that suits you as opposed to making yourself fit a system.

The final strategy I'd like to highlight is one which requires a high risk tolerance and extreme mental discipline. Unlike most of the strategies I usually highlight, this is a counter trend approach and I would not recommend any beginner try this out. At the end of a trend, you'll often see the momentum flag and counter trend forces build up. The force index sometimes works as a leading indicator in such situations and you will see the indicator diverge from price. For example, you'll see price continue upwards while the force index either dips or goes flat. Now, this is the point where every single divergence trader get in and the effect is to usually push price in the trend direction even further because of the greater number of professional traders who fade this strategy. We meanwhile sit tight and watch the force index. They key characteristic to look for is to see whether the indicator retests the previous trend's trend line or support level. I do not mean trend line of the price or S/R level of price but the levels on the indicator itself. These prior levels are where momentum changes happened and its a good bet that the traders involved in making those changes there will be willing to participate again in the opposite direction. Thus as the force index retests those prior levels (on its own curve, NOT the price chart), we enter in a counter trend direction with a stop above or below a logical S/R level. As you can imagine, this involves you shorting or going long very near the top or bottom of the trend against it. This takes serious mental strength to do and requires a fair bit of training. This is why I do not recommend beginners trade this strategy, you'll simply burn yourself out.

The charts in the following pages will illustrate the various strategies we've looked at thus far.

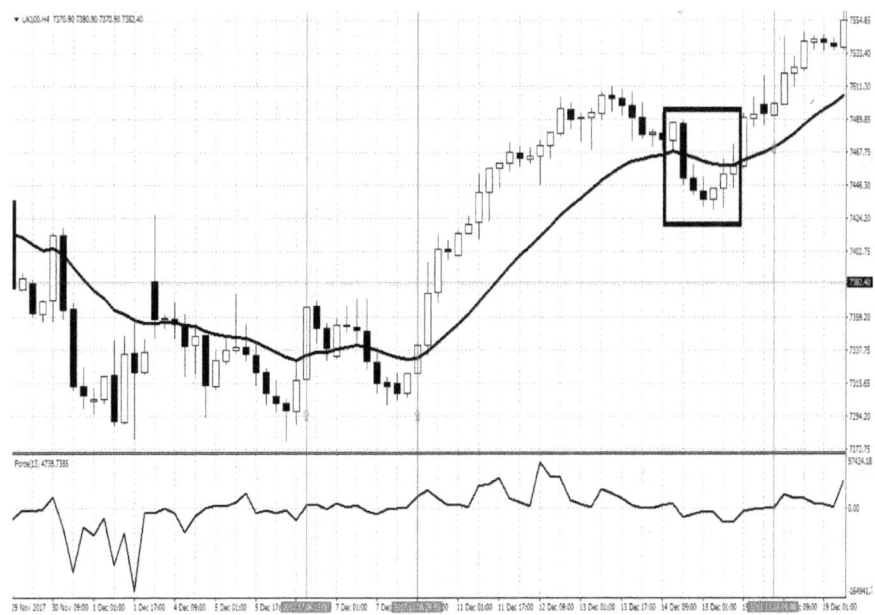

The above chart illustrates a couple different methods by which you can trade the force index. The chart has a 20 EMA plotted on it. The instrument used is the FTSE 100 index. The interval I've used for the indicator is 13 and the time frame is 4 hour chart.

The force index is quite useful for determining trend reversals on any time frame. Here we see at the left of that chart a range which is at the end of a bear trend (not seen). Price stays in this range for a while and I've marked a long entry, indicated by the first vertical line with the arrow beneath it). At this point, we see the force index crossing the 0 level from below into positive territory. The EMA slope is flat. Similarly, the next vertical line also shows a similar logic behind the long entry. Flat EMA but force index crossing past 0 into positive territory. This is an example of a very aggressive way to trade this indicator. Here's my thought process behind this: Price is in a range and I'm reasoning that this range can be a good area for reversal. (Generally a large range following a trend indicates reversal. Please note: the range needs to be large relative to the preceding trend, you cannot blindly apply this to any old range as you please). Since I'm already on the lookout for a reversal, my strategy is to look for a low risk entry and get in on the bull trend as early as possible. This area is low risk since its so close to the bottom anyway while the potential reward is huge since it could result in a bull trend. With this thought process in mind, I decide to become aggressive and trade any bullish indication with my stop below the range bottom. At the first vertical line, I see a strong close above the EMA with the indicator crossing into positive territory. Given my aggressive outlook, I decide to enter despite the EMA staying flat. The second vertical line gives me an even better entry and at this point I just need to wait and watch. If the bull trend doesn't materialize, no matter, my risk is quite small. If it works out, I'll be making a significant amount of profit. As it turns out, it did work out and I'm now on board a nice bull trend from the start.

The rectangle marked in the middle of the chart is a place where most novice traders will get caught out. Either they blindly apply the previously mentioned aggressive approach of they see that the EMA has a slightly downward slope compared to previously and that the indicator has dipped below 0. They'll usually consider this a good place to go short and end up with a loss. The next logical step for them is to blame the indicator for not being good enough. The truth is such traders do not understand that you need to modulate your aggressiveness when entering the market. In this particular situation, we're in the first correction in a bull trend which has just started. This is the last place we want to be going short! So a dip below zero is an insignificant occurrence. If anything we ought to be waiting for the moment the indicator re-crosses the zero level into positive territory so we can get on board the bull trend. This is what the third vertical line is.

Note here that the entry criterion is a bit different from before. The trend is already establish and the first correction has already taken place. Technically, the price could correct back a long way and we could still be in a bull trend. Therefore, my risk of entry here is a bit higher than previously. Therefore, I need a greater number of factors lining up in my favor. This is why, in addition to the positive cross over of the force index, I also look at the slope of the EMA (which is definitely tilting upwards) to make an entry decision. Remember, for the first 2 entries, I didn't consider the EMA slope and decided a strong close above it was good enough. This is because the risk involved at these positions is completely different, not to mention, the reward at this point is lesser than what was on offer at the previous levels simply due to the fact that there previous positions were entered before the trend had even begun.

As you can see, if you apply a little discretion to your trade entry decision, the rewards on offer are far more than a mechanical system. Trading a simple zero crossover system might have got you more entries and a small profit but by taking a step back and assessing the risk reward behind each position, we've made many multiples of profit compared to the mechanical system. This is how a professional thinks and you need to think this way as well if you wish to make big money in the markets. This doesn't mean you don't follow mechanical systems. Just understand their limitations. The flip side is that its easier to get started with a mechanical system than this discretionary method which requires you to do a lot of mental work. You really need to understand risk management and mindset principles to make this work. My recommendation would be to get started with a mechanical system, just pick one of the many I've listed thus far and in my previous book in this series, and simultaneously work on the risk and mindset side of trading. This way, you'll make some money and when you're ready you can level up, so to speak, easily. In my opinion this is the best way to progress.

The daily chart of the FTSE shows how the force index can be used to determine long term trend changes. A prolonged range after a bear trend indicates change is afoot. The timing can be nailed down thanks to this indicator.

The force index decisively pops above 0 into positive territory right around the time the price starts making higher lows. Before the FTSE breaks out of the range, we've already established that accumulation has taken place and we're in a bull trend which will likely last a while.

The period used here for the force index is 100 as discussed previously. Notice how much smoother this line is around the 0 level and relative lack of crossovers.

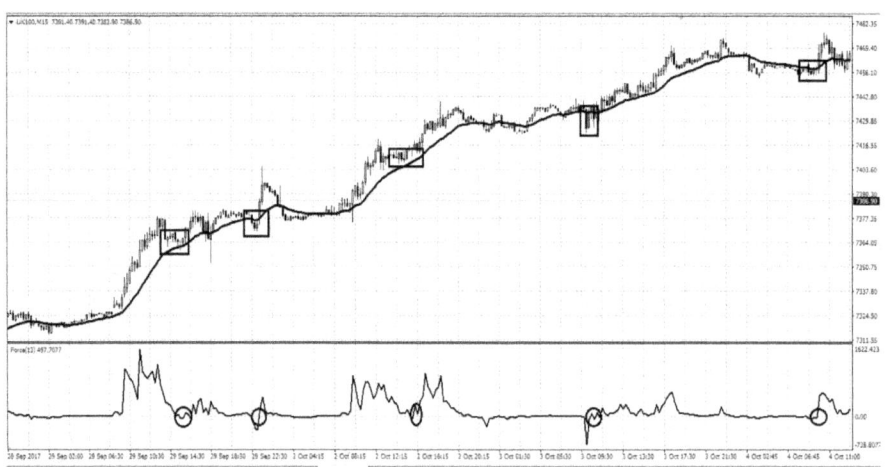

The most effective way to use this indicator is to day trade with it. The chart on top is the hourly chart showing a clear uptrend which we discern via the ema slope. Dropping down to the 15 minute chart of the FTSE, we see multiple moments when the force index crosses zero into positive territory enabling us to spot the end of the pullback and get on board the bull trend. The cross overs are highlighted by circles and the entry points are indicated by the rectangles.

The key is to spot the trend on the higher time frame correctly. You can use an indicator like the ADX for greater accuracy.

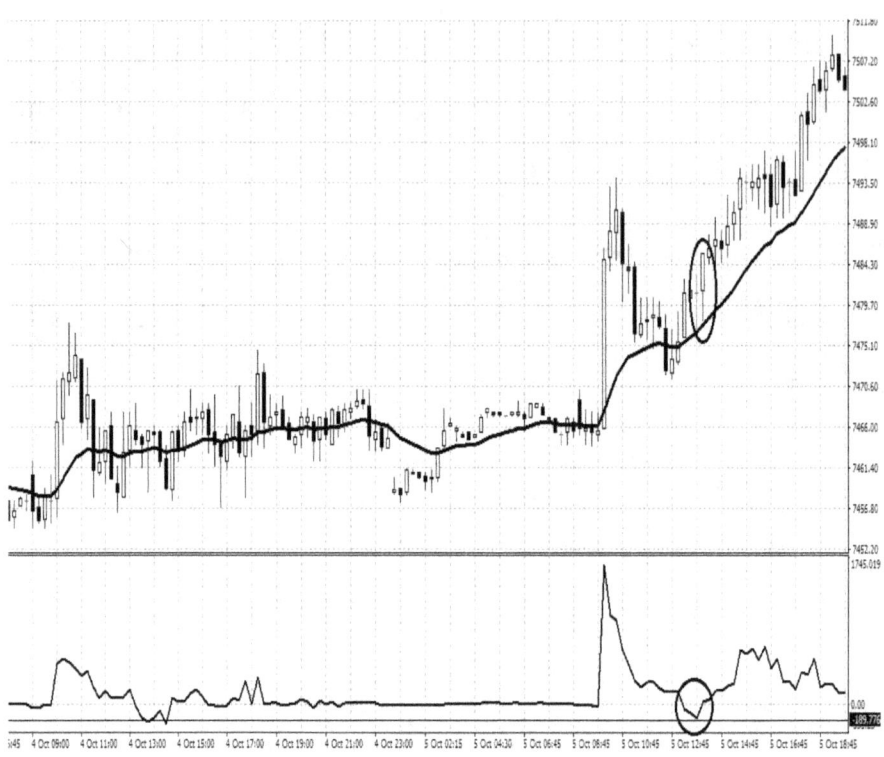

The circles illustrate how to use the force index when an extreme value is registered due to a volume spike. Notice how the indicator works its way back to a previous support level (in the indicator window look at the horizontal line).

Once the indicator bounces up from this line, we enter long (since the move that produced the spike was a bullish bar. Another method is to look at the EMA position vis-a-vis the price bar. In this case the bar is above the EMA and the EMA has a positive slope, all signs of bullishness).

This was on a 15 minute time frame. You won't see many signals like this but when it does occur. Its fairly easy to spot and trade.

An unconventional way of using the force index. Near the end of a bull trend, we see a trend line form on the oscillator. As price moves higher, the indicator forms a lower high which retests the flip side of the trend line. Seeing this, we short the subsequent bar with a stop some distance above based on higher time frame S/R principles.

This is not a strategy you will see present itself very often but it is lucrative when it does so. You will of course need extreme discipline to trade this and I do not recommend beginner traders trade this way.

That concludes our look at the force index. Next up, we take a look at the Williams percent range oscillator.

Chapter 5: William's Percent Range

Developed by Larry Williams, the William's percent range or simply abbreviated as Williams%R or %R even, is an oscillator that behaves and measures much the same things as the previous ones detailed in this book thus far. This is a momentum indicator that is much like the fast stochastic oscillator we saw in the previous book, but the difference is that the scale here is inverted. The respective methods of calculation differ as well as will be evident soon. The readings of this indicator are all negative with thresholds indicating overbought and oversold levels. Indeed, many of the strategies used for the stochastic can be safely used for the %R. Why use this indicator then? Well, this oscillator lacks the smoothing that the stochastic has. Also, due to its relatively lower usage, compared to the stochastic, you will sometimes receive better quality signals. Substituting the %R into strategies which call for the stochastic will sometimes give slightly better results, which is a big deal over a long time period.

This slightly different behavior is mostly observed when a reversal is impending. Indeed, the %R is almost notorious for being able to predict with close to 100% certainty the occurrence of a reversal ahead of time. Most traders will see the oscillator turn away from its extreme points a few bars ahead. This is most likely due to the way in which the indicator is used by most traders allied to the fact that comparatively speaking, other oscillators are used more heavily. As long as such behavior exists, we might as well use it as part of our strategies.

The calculation is as follows:

%R= (Highest High over period -Close)/(Highest High over period- Lowest Low over period) * -100

The terms are self explanatory. The period refers to the look back period native to any indicator. The default value is 14 which can be adjusted depending on the sensitivity you prefer. Visually, the indicator can be seen as a curve which fluctuates between 0 and -100. There will be horizontal lines drawn at -20 and -80 indicating overbought and oversold levels respectively. Just to make this absolutely clear: The negative values do not mean bearishness. One needs to ignore the negative sign and just focus on the numbers. Might sound obvious but when using this in conjunction with other indicators, its a mistake easy and costly enough to make. As can be seen from the calculation, the indicator compares the %R compares the percentage difference between the current close and the relative high and low of the look back period.

The mid level, or -50, often functions as the line of control between bulls and bears. Crossovers often herald changes in momentum. Now a word of caution. Personally, I'm no fan of using indicators like these to predict bullish or bearish changes in trend momentum. Every trader out there uses it in this fashion and there's not much to be gained by using it in the same way as everybody else does. My advice therefore is to leave trend predictions to the trend indicators or use a system like the trend strength method (as detailed in my other books) to help determine true trend momentum and bullish and bearish distribution. This level does bear watching though. If you see enough fake outs and whipsaws in price, you could consider a fading strategy over the short term. After all, many popular indicators are used in this way by professionals, that is, fading the strategy that is most popular or obvious.

Since the strategies you can use this oscillator in and the various methods are extremely similar to other oscillators, mostly the stochastic, there isn't really a great deal to be said strategy wise that hasn't been said before. Therefore, I'll be briefly going over some strategies followed by charts. If this indicator is more to your liking, I suggest perusing the chapter on the stochastic oscillator in the previous book of this series to understand the nuances of the strategies. (There's always a cynic somewhere who'll see this as an up sell. You can choose to re read earlier chapters of this book as well if you so choose.)

As a bound oscillator, the overbought and oversold levels are of primary importance to us. Do note though that a mere move past these levels does not indicate anything. In a strong enough trend, the indicator will remain in oversold or overbought level for quite a while. Therefore, mimicking a strategy we looked at previously, we go long when the indicator crosses the -80 level from below (that is from below -80 to above -80) and we short when the indicator crosses -20 from above (from above -20 to below -20). There is a bit of a twist though. When using this indicator, we do not need price to cross below or above the 20 EMA. In fact, I would suggest making it a rule that to go short, price has to be above the 20 EMA and when going long, price needs to be below the 20 EMA. There's a few reasons for this. First off, as explained previously, the %R has an uncanny ability to predict reversals a few bars beforehand most probably due to the fact that most traders are using this in a very conventional way. Using it in this manner is unconventional and gives you an immediate edge. The second reason is a further play on the unconventionality. How many traders do you think will short an instrument while its above the 20 EMA? Or go long when its below the 20 EMA? Not many. Coupled with the %R, this gives us a greater edge and you will find that this strategy will work most of the time. You will need a few optimizers though.

Firstly, look for price to be approaching a decent S/R level on a higher time frame. For example, if you trade the 60 minute charts, go up to the 4 hour or daily charts to see if price is approaching a major level. Then as it nears the level, go back down to the 60 minute and watch for the entry condition to be fulfilled. Place your stop above or below the S/R or at any logical point you see on the chart. Target a reward of 2R at least with this strategy.

Another unconventional way to use this indicator is to watch it for signs of flagging or decreasing momentum. A universal characteristic of trends is the ability of the with trend players to constantly keep pushing it in the required direction. This force prints as repeated breaches of the overbought or oversold levels on the %R, or indeed, any oscillator. If we see a break in this pattern, that is, the indicator after a succession of breaches into the extreme levels, fails to do so, this is a great sign of momentum beginning in the opposite direction. An entry opposite to the direction of the recently concluded trend is a great way to take advantage of this. The downside of this strategy is deciding stop loss levels since you will often find that this occurs not near the top but near the start of trends but far enough away from the extreme points. My suggestion is to take it on a case by case basis and target a minimum of 2R.

The preceding paragraphs are unconventional ways to use this indicator. Their strength and profitability lies in them being exactly that. There are of course very conventional ways to use the indicator but these strategies have already been covered and it would be extremely repetitive to go over them again, not to mention a waste of your time since you've already been exposed to the ethos of a conventional oscillator strategy.

The charts on the next few pages illustrate the strategies I've highlighted.

The above chart is of the NZDUSD on the H4 time frame. The indicator setting is 14 periods. As you can see, this produces a very sensitive line which throws up a number of entry signals (indicated in the price chart by rectangles). The solid horizontal lines at the top and bottom are daily, that is higher time frame, S/R levels. These are quite strong levels which have been respected in the past. Since, the dates have not been obscured, you can check these levels yourself and as such I will not be highlighting the HTF chart here.

The boxes satisfy all the entry signals and as you can see there is a mix of both with trend and counter trend signals. I'm not an advocate of beginners taking counter trend signals but in this case, given the quality of this strategy, I will recommend it with a caveat. If you are entering counter trend, make sure you have a decent S/R level close by. The reason I'm saying this is because there are a few signals above which are counter trend but don't have an obvious S/R close by. Its best to stay away from such signals. Even better, use a trend indicator and only trade counter trend when the trend strength becomes weaker. Note: Technically the big reversals occurring near the solid lines are counter trend. I'm not including such signals as part of the caveat. If you see a signal form near a higher time frame S/R level, that's a high quality signal and you must enter with a conservative stop loss level no matter the direction.

You will see that price doesn't respect the S/R level in a clean and clear manner. This seems to be the case because I've represented the levels as a single horizontal line. In reality there is an area of tolerance around these lines which represents a zone. Always place your stop beyond the extremities of this zone and you'll be fine. Even if the odd trade does get stopped out you will still make money with this in the long run.

I recommend covering the chart with a piece of paper and going over it bar by bar for a greater understanding.

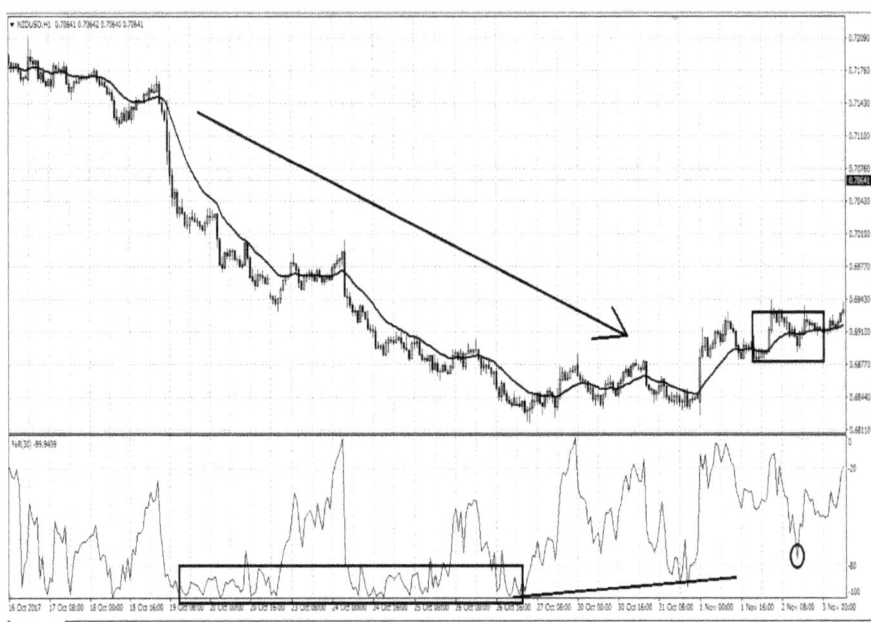

Notice how the NZDUSD, while in a bear trend, has no problem pushing the %R values below -20 repeatedly to the minimum value. Note though as momentum flags, the indicator forms a higher low and finally doesn't make it back below the level.

For this kind of momentum signals, you're better off using a higher look back period. In this case I've used 30. Play around with it and see which one fits you best.

This concludes our look at the %R. Next up, we'll look at how to put all of this together and in the process try to summarize what successful trading processes entail.

Chapter 6: I've Picked My Indicators. Now What?

You now have two books worth of indicators to pick and choose from. Some of you will do the sensible thing and gone away to practice and play around with them to see which ones fit you best. Some of you may go a step further and back test the strategies and tweak some of them to suit you better. Well, what ever scenario fits you, I have some good news and bad news. The good news is this: You will make money using these methods. The bad news is this: 95% of you reading this book will be unable to keep the money you make over the long run.

There's a number of reasons for this, most of them relating to a lack of understanding of risk and mindset management. I'll explore these in significant detail in a separate book. For now, I want to highlight another reason you're likely to lose money using these methods (as if there weren't enough already): Professional and experienced traders. Now, I don't want you to think the professional traders out there are rubbing their hands in glee everyday thinking of ripping you off. This is simply not the case. What I'm trying to say is, as beginner traders once most of you start making money, you will get lazy and fail to develop your skills. This laziness is what will cost you in the long run and cause you to donate your profits right back. Its no good saying "That's not me" because every single successful trader out there (yes, myself included) has done this and has paid the price for doing so. Those who don't fall in this trap are truly exceptional and far from the norm.

So how do you keep developing your skills? A better question to ask is: What is the process of becoming a successful trader? Well, that's what I'm ultimately trying to educate you on through all of my books. Successful trading is about a lot more than the ability to make money. It involves keeping it and becoming so comfortable with it that the money simply doesn't register whether you're winning or losing. Here's a fun fact: During my professional career, I had periods of up to 10 months where I lost money. 10 months of constantly losing at the end of the month. How many of you reading this have had the discipline to stick to something that was giving you losses for 10 days forget months? This isn't something unique to me, every professional and successful trader goes through this. So how does one handle such periods?

The answer is by developing and sticking to a process rigidly. The process has multiple elements to it namely:

- Mindset awareness
- Mental toughness and training
- Risk management
- Risk analytics and assessment
- Technical ability
- Execution mechanics
- Post trade awareness
- Business viability planning
- Training and skill improvement goals

In the next few paragraphs, I'm going to talk about that final bullet point. Most traders make the mistake, in my opinion, of picking a complex strategy or a strategy that requires an immense amount of mental discipline to pull off right at the beginning. According to me, the path which as the shortest distance to success begins by picking a very simple strategy where most of the work is done for you. This means, if you're starting out, you need to pick a purely mechanical strategy. You back test it and develop discipline by trading it on demo and live. Meanwhile, you need to avoid the pitfall of successful trading that most struggling traders fall into: laziness. You need to keep working on your skills, all the bullet points highlighted above, by practicing more and more advanced techniques. This means you transition from a purely mechanical system to a system which requires you to make some subjective calls. You keep increasing the level of subjectivity, while still keeping your indicators open and using them as an aid. This way, if you find yourself losing money as you increase subjectivity or discretion in your system, you can always revert to the previous version which was making you money.

Thus, you're making it easier mentally on yourself to improve and you receive the boost of confidence that success brings you. The final step is letting go of the indicators and trading the charts just by themselves. This is how a professional trades by the way. Traders working for a bank or a proprietary shop aren't sitting there waiting for an indicator to give them an entry signal. Neither are they waiting for some pattern to form which consists of 1 or 2 bars or "fakeys/flakeys" whatever you want to call them. This is why in my other books on forex and stock trading, I advocate the usage of indicators along with a slightly discretionary system at the start. As you get more advanced, I teach you how to read a price chart by itself. There is no better way than trading a price chart by itself since interpreting price is what we're trying to do. Its why we use indicators after all.

My advice to you therefore is to pick and choose your indicators and use it mechanically so as to make some money but recognize that you need to develop your skills to a point where you don't need indicators any more. For those of you who aren't comfortable with any of the indicators I've illustrated thus far, don't worry, there are more books in this series where I break down other types of indicators like the Fibonacci and others which don't really conform to any easy category.

I hope you found this book useful and now understand that the entry decision is but one of many steps in a successful trading process. I wish you the best of luck in your journey and urge you to check out my other books on the subject. I know for a fact that you will not have read anyone else approaching trading in the manner I do and I know your skills and mindset will benefit immensely.

Lastly, if you enjoyed this book or found it helpful, please do leave a review on Amazon, I'll appreciate it very much.

www.ingramcontent.com/pod-product-compliance
Lightning Source LLC
Chambersburg PA
CBHW052334220526
45472CB00001B/417